FISH AND FOWL

EASY AND AWESOME
SANDWICHES

for
KIDS

written by
**ALISON
DEERING**

illustrated by
**BOB
LENTZ**

CAPSTONE PRESS
a capstone imprint

TO MY DAD, WHO TAUGHT ME THE BEAUTY OF A GREAT
LUNCH SANDWICH, AND TO MY MOM, WHO STILL MAKES
ME SANDWICHES NOW. — AD

TO THE SAUCEMAN. SORRY THERE ISN'T MORE RANCH
DRESSING IN HERE. — BL

Savvy Books are published by Capstone Press,
1710 Roe Crest Drive, North Mankato, Minnesota 56003
www.mycapstone.com

Library of Congress Cataloging-in-Publication Data

Names: Deering, Alison, author.
Title: Fish and fowl : easy and awesome sandwiches for kids / by Alison Deering.
Description: North Mankato, Minnesota : Capstone Press, [2017] | Series:
    Savvy. Between the bread | Audience: Age 9–13. | Audience: Grade 4–6. |
    Includes bibliographical references and index.
Identifiers: LCCN 2017008312 | ISBN 9781515739203 (library hardcover)
Subjects: LCSH: Cooking (Fish)—Juvenile literature. | Cooking (Poultry) |
    Cooking (Game) | Sandwiches—Juvenile literature. | LCGFT: Cookbooks.
Classification: LCC TX747 .D44 2017 | DDC 641.84—dc23
LC record available at https://lccn.loc.gov/2017008312

Designer: Bob Lentz
Creative Director: Heather Kindseth
Production Specialist: Tori Abraham

Printed in the United States of America.
010373F17.

TABLE OF CONTENTS

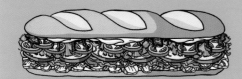

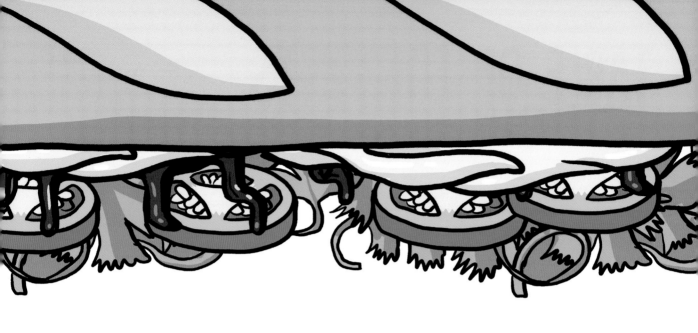

INTRODUCTION

(AKA WHAT IS A SANDWICH)

What is a sandwich? According to the United States Department of Agriculture, the "Product must contain at least 35 percent cooked meat and no more than 50 percent bread." The dictionary is slightly more open-minded, describing a sandwich as "two or more slices of bread or a split roll having a filling in between."

The good news is that filling can be whatever you want it to be — chicken, fish, veggies, cheese, you name it! This between-the-bread guide is packed full of recipes to help you take your fish and fowl offerings to the next level. Bookend your kitchen creation with the bread of your choosing — wheat, white, rye . . . we even encourage waffles as sandwich bases.

The beauty and genius of a delicious sandwich is that YOU as the chef and creator can make it anything you want it to be. And with this guidebook, you'll learn how to build the best sandwiches ever, no red meat required.

TURKEY SWISS ROLLUP

If it doesn't exist between two slices of bread is it really a sandwich? That's a question for another time, but in this instance, we say yes! Rollup, wrap, sandwich-on-the-go — whatever you call it, this handheld turkey and Swiss treat is easy to make and even easier to eat. Use whatever type of tortilla or wrap you'd like (plain, whole wheat, sundried tomato, spinach, etc.), add the fillings, and wrap it up!

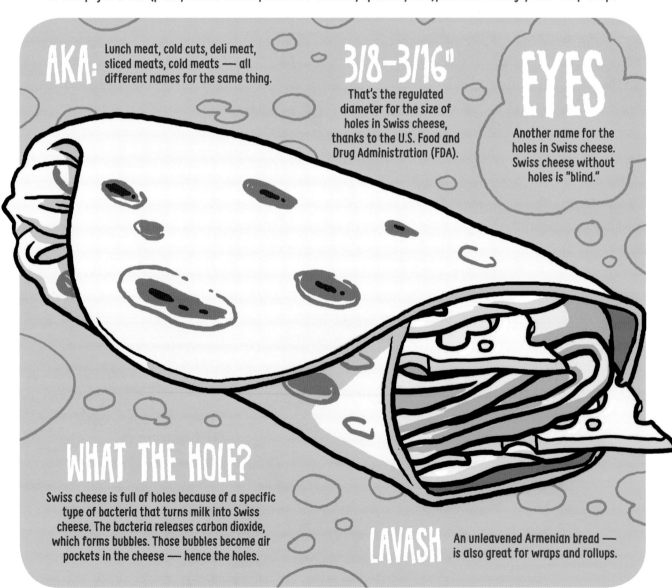

AKA: Lunch meat, cold cuts, deli meat, sliced meats, cold meats — all different names for the same thing.

3/8–3/16" That's the regulated diameter for the size of holes in Swiss cheese, thanks to the U.S. Food and Drug Administration (FDA).

EYES Another name for the holes in Swiss cheese. Swiss cheese without holes is "blind."

WHAT THE HOLE? Swiss cheese is full of holes because of a specific type of bacteria that turns milk into Swiss cheese. The bacteria releases carbon dioxide, which forms bubbles. Those bubbles become air pockets in the cheese — hence the holes.

LAVASH An unleavened Armenian bread — is also great for wraps and rollups.

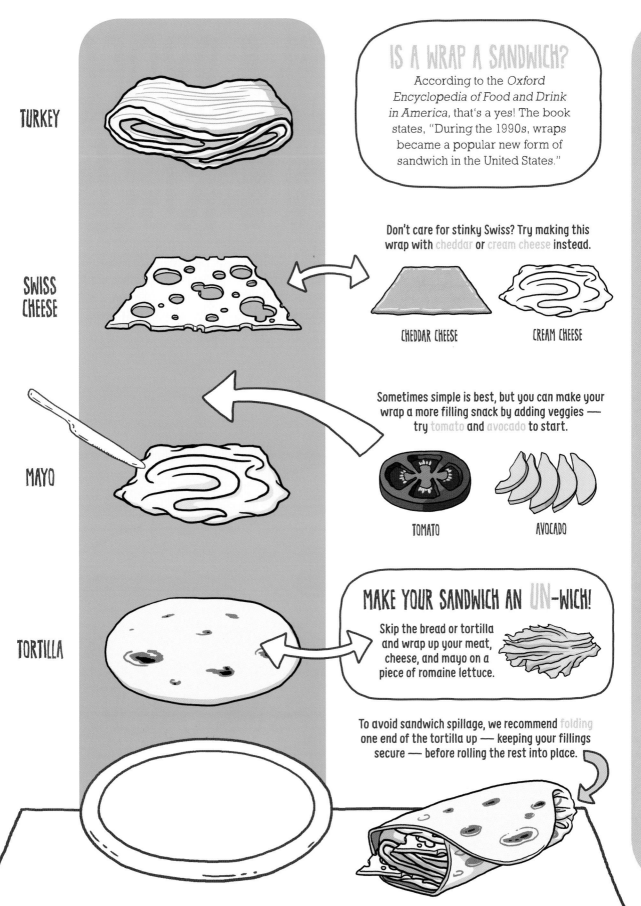

TURKEY

SWISS CHEESE

MAYO

TORTILLA

IS A WRAP A SANDWICH?

According to the *Oxford Encyclopedia of Food and Drink in America*, that's a yes! The book states, "During the 1990s, wraps became a popular new form of sandwich in the United States."

Don't care for stinky Swiss? Try making this wrap with cheddar or cream cheese instead.

CHEDDAR CHEESE

CREAM CHEESE

Sometimes simple is best, but you can make your wrap a more filling snack by adding veggies — try tomato and avocado to start.

TOMATO

AVOCADO

MAKE YOUR SANDWICH AN UN-WICH!

Skip the bread or tortilla and wrap up your meat, cheese, and mayo on a piece of romaine lettuce.

To avoid sandwich spillage, we recommend folding one end of the tortilla up — keeping your fillings secure — before rolling the rest into place.

CHICKEN BROCCOLI ROLLUP

This chicken broccoli rollup uses a flour tortilla in place of bread. Just roll up your ingredients and you're ready to go! You can eat this "sandwich" cold, or pop it in the oven to heat things up. If you're eating it cold, we suggest adding hummus or cream cheese and leaving the broccoli raw. If you plan to bake it, stick with shredded cheddar and cook your broccoli before you add it to the wrap.

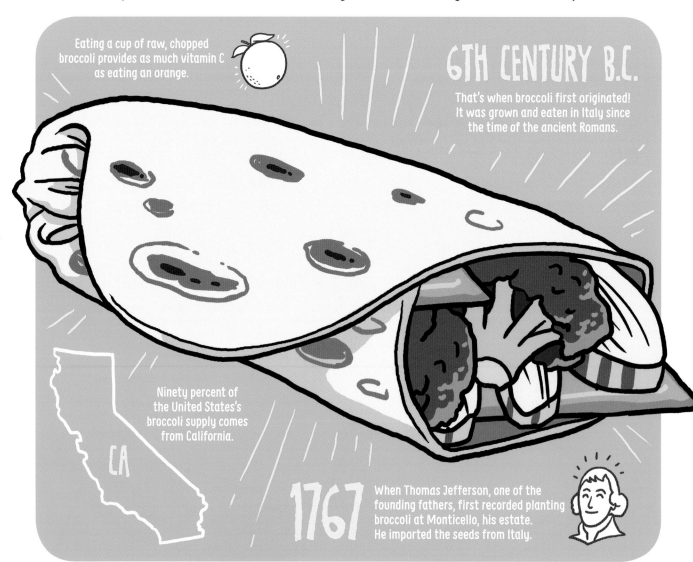

Eating a cup of raw, chopped broccoli provides as much vitamin C as eating an orange.

6TH CENTURY B.C.

That's when broccoli first originated! It was grown and eaten in Italy since the time of the ancient Romans.

Ninety percent of the United States's broccoli supply comes from California.

CA

1767 When Thomas Jefferson, one of the founding fathers, first recorded planting broccoli at Monticello, his estate. He imported the seeds from Italy.

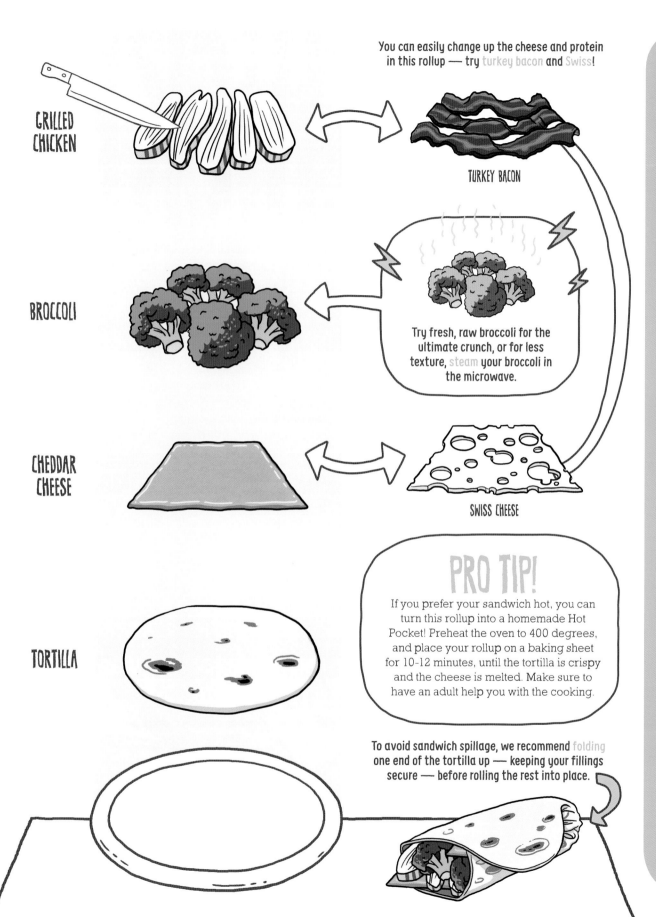

You can easily change up the cheese and protein in this rollup — try turkey bacon and Swiss!

GRILLED CHICKEN

TURKEY BACON

BROCCOLI

Try fresh, raw broccoli for the ultimate crunch, or for less texture, steam your broccoli in the microwave.

CHEDDAR CHEESE

SWISS CHEESE

PRO TIP!

If you prefer your sandwich hot, you can turn this rollup into a homemade Hot Pocket! Preheat the oven to 400 degrees, and place your rollup on a baking sheet for 10-12 minutes, until the tortilla is crispy and the cheese is melted. Make sure to have an adult help you with the cooking.

TORTILLA

To avoid sandwich spillage, we recommend folding one end of the tortilla up — keeping your fillings secure — before rolling the rest into place.

PESTO CHICKEN

Whether you're putting it on pizza, using it as a dipping sauce, or spreading it on a sandwich, pesto is one perfect creation. It also gives leftover chicken new life when slathered on Italian bread and paired with creamy mozzarella. Try making your own pesto, especially in the summer, when fresh basil is easy to find, making this scrumptious spreadable even more approachable.

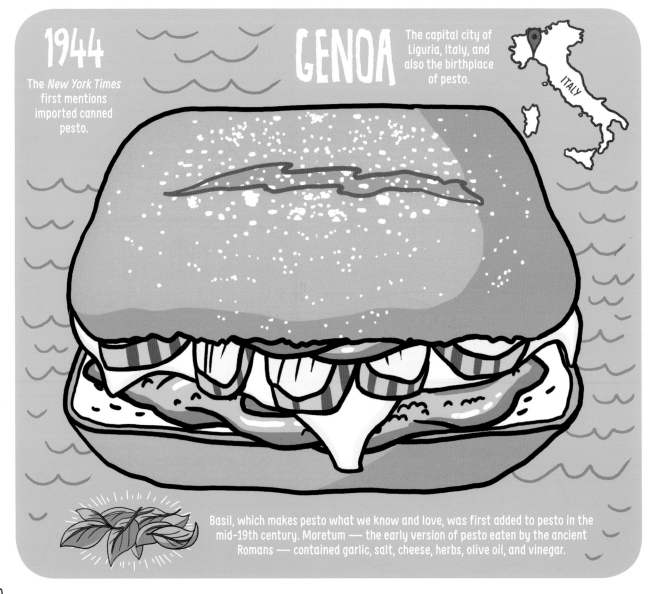

1944

The *New York Times* first mentions imported canned pesto.

GENOA

The capital city of Liguria, Italy, and also the birthplace of pesto.

ITALY

Basil, which makes pesto what we know and love, was first added to pesto in the mid-19th century. Moretum — the early version of pesto eaten by the ancient Romans — contained garlic, salt, cheese, herbs, olive oil, and vinegar.

CIABATTA BREAD

PESTO

GRILLED CHICKEN

MOZZARELLA CHEESE

PESTO

CIABATTA BREAD

You can buy pesto at the store, but it's also easy to make if you're feeling inspired.

HOMEMADE PESTO

2 cups fresh basil
1/4 cup olive oil
1/4 cup pine nuts
1/4 cup parmesan cheese
1 clove garlic
salt
pepper

Place all your ingredients into a blender or food processor and blend until smooth. (Make sure you have a grown-up's permission before using the blender.) Store the extra in a tightly sealed container in your fridge.

Pesto is traditionally made with basil and pine nuts, but this delicious spread can also be made with a variety of other ingredients. Try experimenting with some of the following:

WALNUTS   ALMONDS   PECANS

PEAS   ARUGULA   SPINACH

This sandwich can be served hot or cold. If you plan to grill it, we suggest swapping out the ciabatta for wheat bread to make things easier.

FRIED CHICKEN

Fried chicken is the ultimate comfort food, and now you can enjoy it in sandwich form! You don't have to fire up the deep fryer either — this easy-to-make (and even easier-to-enjoy) sandwich is made using leftover chicken fingers, which are just as delicious cold. (If you prefer yours hot — or you're fresh out of leftovers — you can easily heat some up in the oven. Just make sure you have a grownup's help or permission.)

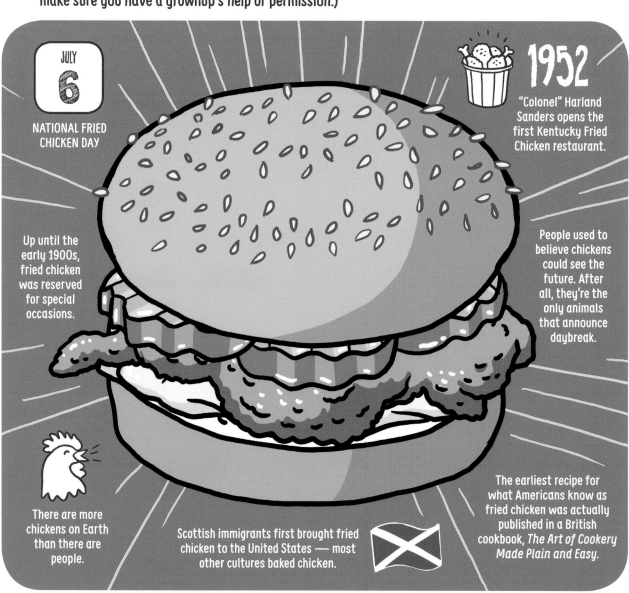

JULY
6

NATIONAL FRIED CHICKEN DAY

1952

"Colonel" Harland Sanders opens the first Kentucky Fried Chicken restaurant.

Up until the early 1900s, fried chicken was reserved for special occasions.

People used to believe chickens could see the future. After all, they're the only animals that announce daybreak.

There are more chickens on Earth than there are people.

Scottish immigrants first brought fried chicken to the United States — most other cultures baked chicken.

The earliest recipe for what Americans know as fried chicken was actually published in a British cookbook, *The Art of Cookery Made Plain and Easy*.

HAMBURGER
BUN

PICKLES

FRIED
CHICKEN

MAYO

HAMBURGER
BUN

CHEESE PLEASE!
Add a slice of
American cheese
to your fried chicken
sandwich to take it
up a notch.

PICK YOUR PICKLE!
Dill pickles, sweet pickles, or spicy pickles
can all be used on a fried chicken sandwich.
The choice is yours!

TURKEY BACON!

You can customize this sandwich
any way you like — try adding these
to start!

BBQ SAUCE   HONEY MUSTARD

COLESLAW

Ready to go full-on southern comfort
with your fried chicken sandwich?
Add mashed potatoes to the mix! You
can serve them on the side, or add
them to your sandwich.

FRIED CHICKEN

BUFFALO CHICKEN

Ready to spice things up? A kick of hot, spicy buffalo sauce takes this chicken sandwich up a notch. While buffalo sauce is most commonly associated with buffalo wings, the flavor is just as good when eaten between bread. Lettuce, sour cream, and blue cheese can all help balance the heat a little bit, but how spicy your sandwich turns out is up to you.

1964 NY
Buffalo wings are created in Buffalo, New York, by Theresa Bellissimo at the Anchor Bar.

JULY 29
NATIONAL CHICKEN WING DAY

90
The number of buffalo wings the average American eats each year.

444
The record for most buffalo wings eaten — this took 26 minutes.

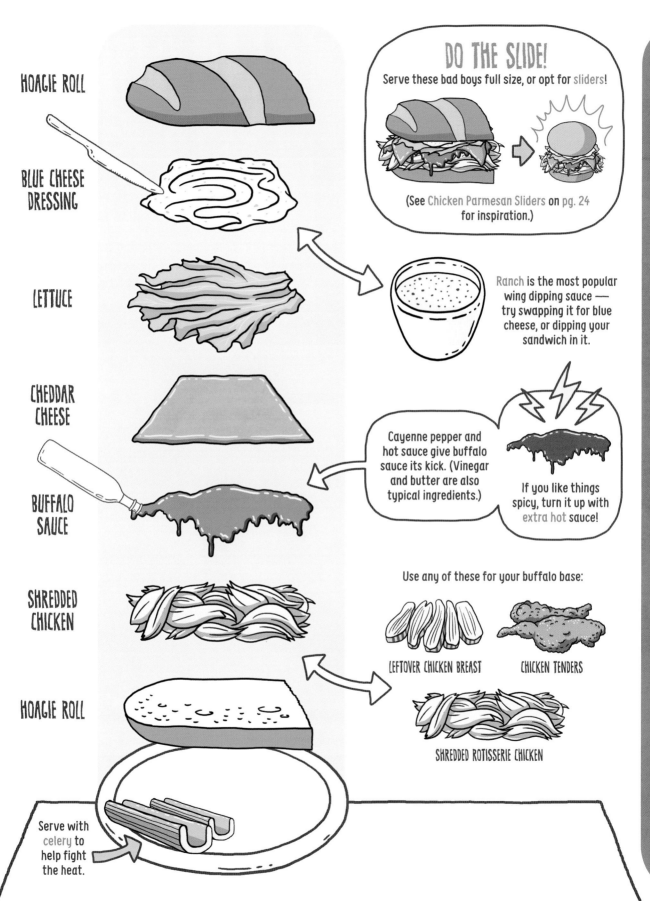

HOAGIE ROLL

BLUE CHEESE DRESSING

LETTUCE

CHEDDAR CHEESE

BUFFALO SAUCE

SHREDDED CHICKEN

HOAGIE ROLL

DO THE SLIDE!

Serve these bad boys full size, or opt for sliders!

(See Chicken Parmesan Sliders on pg. 24 for inspiration.)

Ranch is the most popular wing dipping sauce — try swapping it for blue cheese, or dipping your sandwich in it.

Cayenne pepper and hot sauce give buffalo sauce its kick. (Vinegar and butter are also typical ingredients.)

If you like things spicy, turn it up with extra hot sauce!

Use any of these for your buffalo base:

LEFTOVER CHICKEN BREAST

CHICKEN TENDERS

SHREDDED ROTISSERIE CHICKEN

Serve with celery to help fight the heat.

BUFFALO CHICKEN

TURKEY LEFTOVERS ("THE GOBBLER")

Stuffing your face with turkey is quite possibly the best part of Thanksgiving — or any holiday, for that matter. But second best? The leftovers, hands down! And now you have the perfect sandwich to incorporate all your holiday favorites — leftover turkey, gravy, stuffing, and cranberry sauce — into one mouthwatering meal. Now that's something to be thankful for.

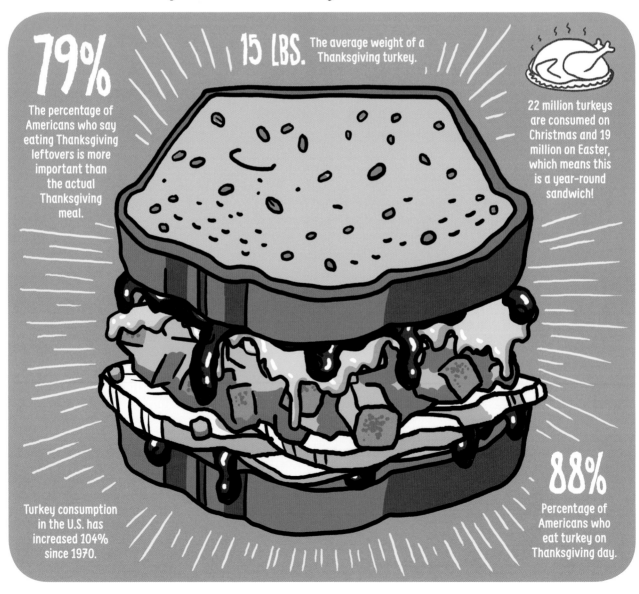

79%
The percentage of Americans who say eating Thanksgiving leftovers is more important than the actual Thanksgiving meal.

15 LBS. The average weight of a Thanksgiving turkey.

22 million turkeys are consumed on Christmas and 19 million on Easter, which means this is a year-round sandwich!

Turkey consumption in the U.S. has increased 104% since 1970.

88%
Percentage of Americans who eat turkey on Thanksgiving day.

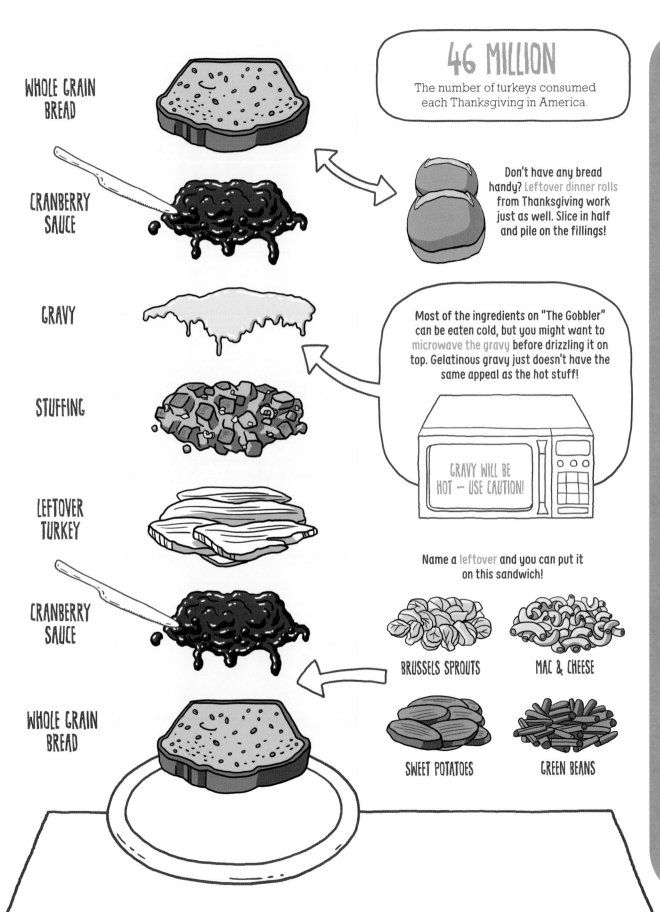

WHOLE GRAIN
BREAD

CRANBERRY
SAUCE

GRAVY

STUFFING

LEFTOVER
TURKEY

CRANBERRY
SAUCE

WHOLE GRAIN
BREAD

46 MILLION
The number of turkeys consumed each Thanksgiving in America.

Don't have any bread handy? Leftover dinner rolls from Thanksgiving work just as well. Slice in half and pile on the fillings!

Most of the ingredients on "The Gobbler" can be eaten cold, but you might want to microwave the gravy before drizzling it on top. Gelatinous gravy just doesn't have the same appeal as the hot stuff!

GRAVY WILL BE
HOT — USE CAUTION!

Name a leftover and you can put it on this sandwich!

BRUSSELS SPROUTS

MAC & CHEESE

SWEET POTATOES

GREEN BEANS

CHICKEN — AND — WAFFLES

Is it breakfast? Is it lunch? Who knows! We don't have all the answers — all we know is that it's delicious. This southern staple is equal parts sweet and savory; and the nooks and crannies in the waffle — perfect for capturing cheese or maple syrup — don't hurt either. Chicken and waffles, a match made in culinary heaven!

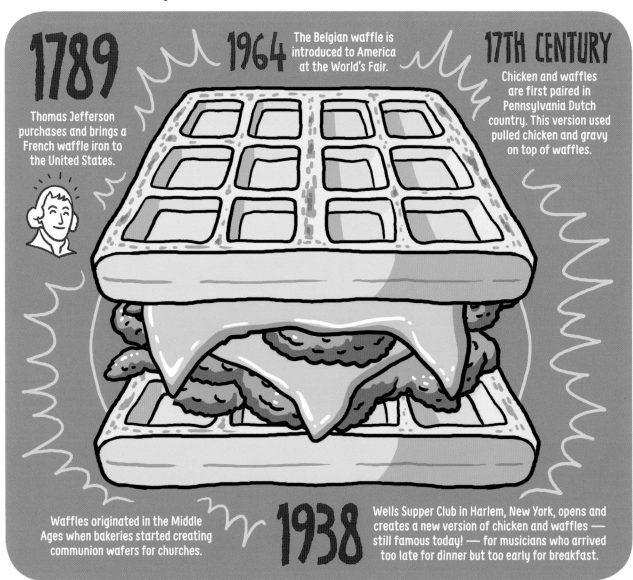

1789

Thomas Jefferson purchases and brings a French waffle iron to the United States.

1964

The Belgian waffle is introduced to America at the World's Fair.

17TH CENTURY

Chicken and waffles are first paired in Pennsylvania Dutch country. This version used pulled chicken and gravy on top of waffles.

Waffles originated in the Middle Ages when bakeries started creating communion wafers for churches.

1938

Wells Supper Club in Harlem, New York, opens and creates a new version of chicken and waffles — still famous today! — for musicians who arrived too late for dinner but too early for breakfast.

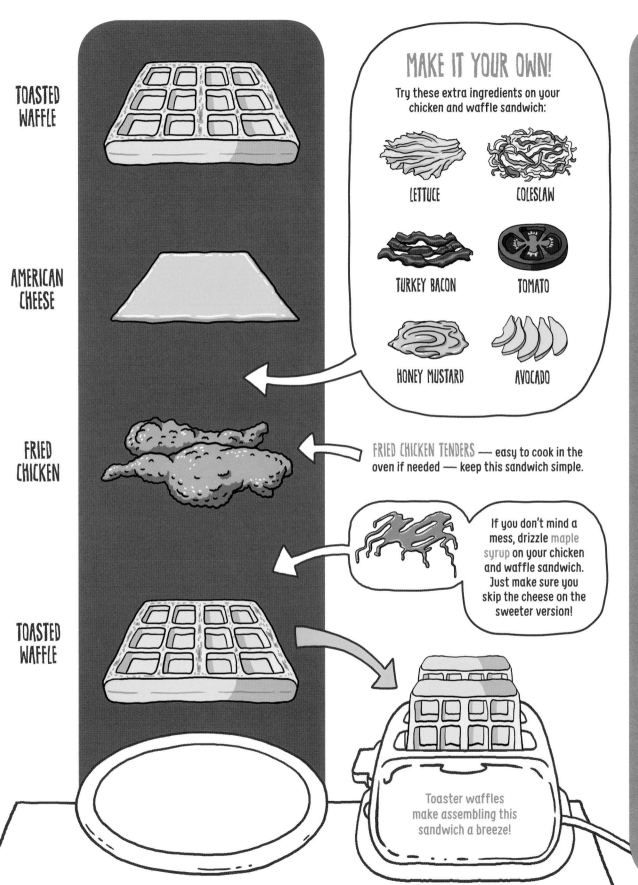

TOASTED WAFFLE

AMERICAN CHEESE

FRIED CHICKEN

TOASTED WAFFLE

MAKE IT YOUR OWN!

Try these extra ingredients on your chicken and waffle sandwich:

LETTUCE

COLESLAW

TURKEY BACON

TOMATO

HONEY MUSTARD

AVOCADO

FRIED CHICKEN TENDERS — easy to cook in the oven if needed — keep this sandwich simple.

If you don't mind a mess, drizzle maple syrup on your chicken and waffle sandwich. Just make sure you skip the cheese on the sweeter version!

Toaster waffles make assembling this sandwich a breeze!

BAGEL AND LOX

Biting into a soft, chewy bagel in the morning is the ultimate delight. Smear on some cream cheese, add some lox, salty capers, tomato, and red onion, and you've got yourself a real breakfast sandwich! You can serve this sandwich open-faced, as is traditional, or put the top on if you prefer your bagel and lox with a lid. Feeling extra hungry? Use both halves of the bagel as their own individual sandwiches.

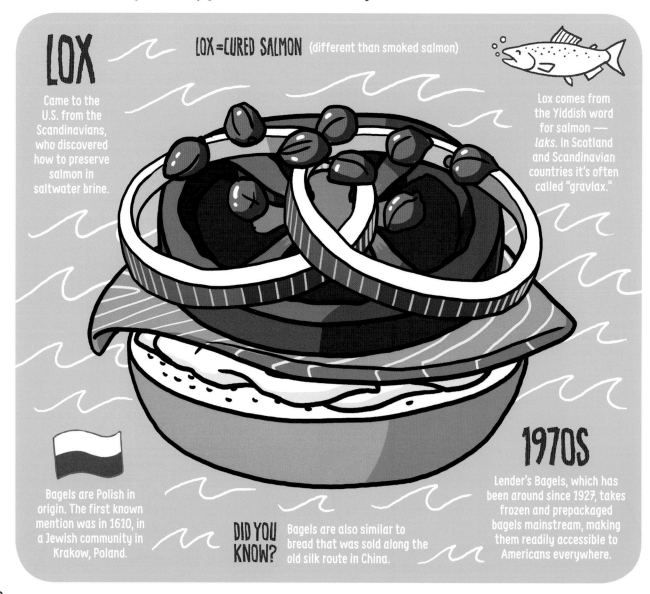

LOX

LOX = CURED SALMON (different than smoked salmon)

Came to the U.S. from the Scandinavians, who discovered how to preserve salmon in saltwater brine.

Lox comes from the Yiddish word for salmon — *laks*. In Scotland and Scandinavian countries it's often called "gravlax."

Bagels are Polish in origin. The first known mention was in 1610, in a Jewish community in Krakow, Poland.

DID YOU KNOW? Bagels are also similar to bread that was sold along the old silk route in China.

1970S

Lender's Bagels, which has been around since 1927, takes frozen and prepackaged bagels mainstream, making them readily accessible to Americans everywhere.

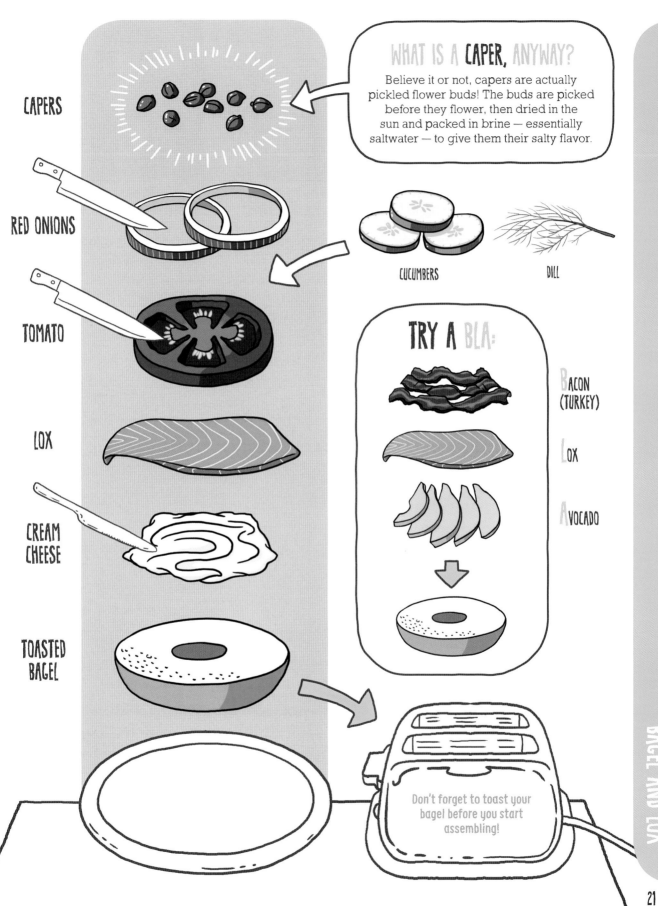

CAPERS

RED ONIONS

TOMATO

LOX

CREAM
CHEESE

TOASTED
BAGEL

WHAT IS A **CAPER**, ANYWAY?

Believe it or not, capers are actually pickled flower buds! The buds are picked before they flower, then dried in the sun and packed in brine — essentially saltwater — to give them their salty flavor.

CUCUMBERS

DILL

TRY A BLA:

BACON
(TURKEY)

LOX

AVOCADO

Don't forget to toast your bagel before you start assembling!

FRIED FISH

The fried fish sandwich can be found from the Atlantic to the Pacific in the U.S., and why not?! It's easy, delicious, and satisfying. You can use oven-baked fried fish fillets as the meat in this sandwich. Just have an adult help you with the oven, and follow the cooking instructions on the package. Walleye, cod, and halibut are great choices for fish, but any type of fried whitefish will do.

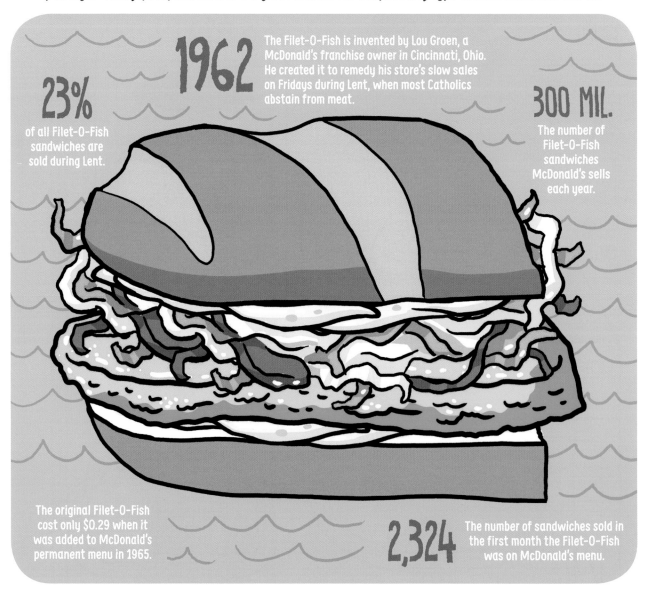

23%
of all Filet-O-Fish sandwiches are sold during Lent.

1962
The Filet-O-Fish is invented by Lou Groen, a McDonald's franchise owner in Cincinnati, Ohio. He created it to remedy his store's slow sales on Fridays during Lent, when most Catholics abstain from meat.

300 MIL.
The number of Filet-O-Fish sandwiches McDonald's sells each year.

The original Filet-O-Fish cost only $0.29 when it was added to McDonald's permanent menu in 1965.

2,324
The number of sandwiches sold in the first month the Filet-O-Fish was on McDonald's menu.

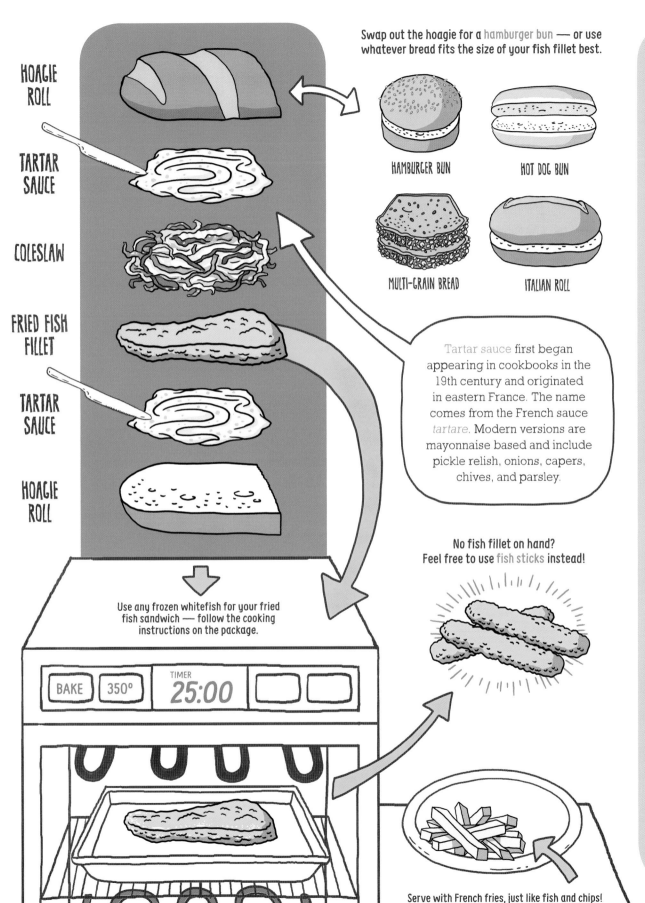

HOAGIE ROLL

TARTAR SAUCE

COLESLAW

FRIED FISH FILLET

TARTAR SAUCE

HOAGIE ROLL

Swap out the hoagie for a hamburger bun — or use whatever bread fits the size of your fish fillet best.

HAMBURGER BUN

HOT DOG BUN

MULTI-GRAIN BREAD

ITALIAN ROLL

Tartar sauce first began appearing in cookbooks in the 19th century and originated in eastern France. The name comes from the French sauce *tartare*. Modern versions are mayonnaise based and include pickle relish, onions, capers, chives, and parsley.

Use any frozen whitefish for your fried fish sandwich — follow the cooking instructions on the package.

BAKE 350° TIMER 25:00

No fish fillet on hand? Feel free to use fish sticks instead!

Serve with French fries, just like fish and chips!

CHICKEN PARMESAN SLIDERS

Why eat one sandwich when you could eat multiple mini sandwiches? That's the beauty of sliders. The same full-sized sandwich you love shrunk down to nearly bite-sized. Sliders are perfect for a party or to enjoy on your own. And while you *could* make just one, why would you? We suggest prepping a pan of these sliders so you can eat — or share — as many as you'd like. (Just remember, most mouths have a one-slider-at-a-time limit.)

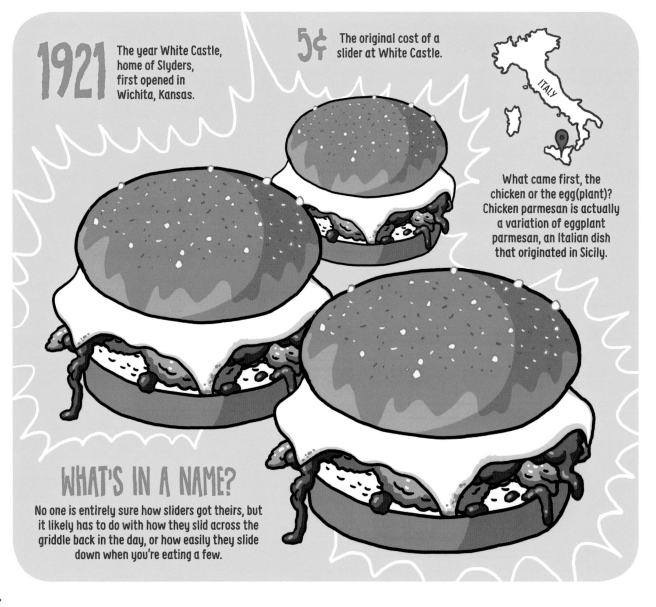

1921 The year White Castle, home of Slyders, first opened in Wichita, Kansas.

5¢ The original cost of a slider at White Castle.

ITALY

What came first, the chicken or the egg(plant)? Chicken parmesan is actually a variation of eggplant parmesan, an Italian dish that originated in Sicily.

WHAT'S IN A NAME?

No one is entirely sure how sliders got theirs, but it likely has to do with how they slid across the griddle back in the day, or how easily they slide down when you're eating a few.

SLIDER BUN

Brush the top with melted butter, then dust with garlic powder and italian seasoning.

PARMESAN CHEESE

Chicken Parmesan Sliders are just one option — you can use this same method to make any other type of slider as well! Try pulled chicken sliders with BBQ sauce, or turkey burger sliders.

MOZZARELLA CHEESE

MARINARA SAUCE

If you don't want fried chicken, substitute leftover chicken breast or rotisserie chicken.

CHICKEN TENDER

SLIDER BUN

Ready to make your sliders in bulk? With a grownup's help, preheat the oven to 375 degrees. Cut your slider buns in half and place the bottom halves in a baking dish or tray. Layer on all your ingredients and place the half of your slider buns on top. Brush on melted butter, garlic, and seasonings, and bake for 20 minutes.

OR!

Assemble the bottom half of your slider (up to the mozzarella) and have an adult help you put it under the broiler to melt the cheese.

TIMER
2:50   BROIL   HI

Then top it with parmesan and the top bun.

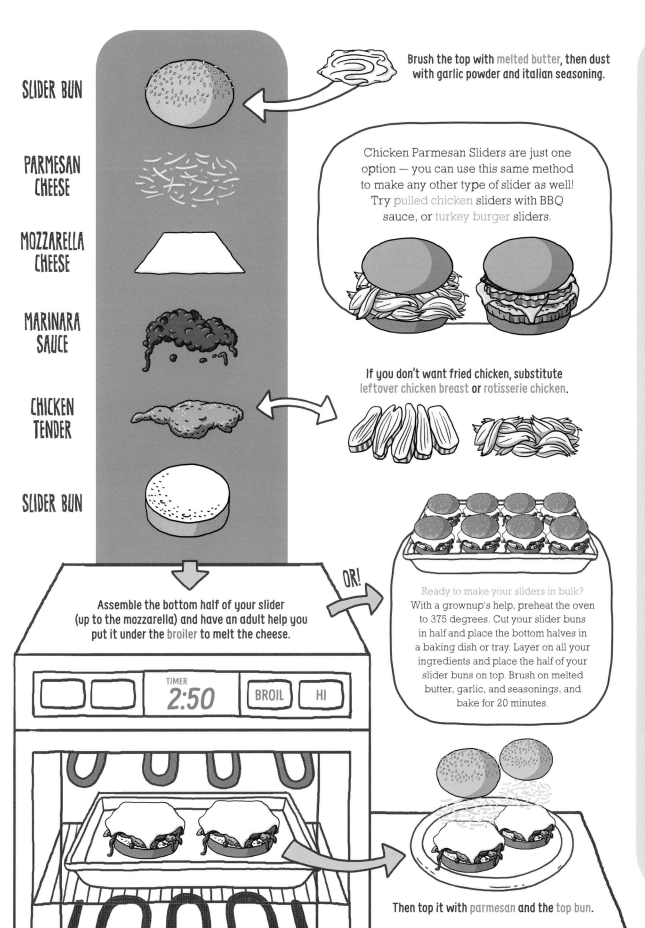

CHICKEN APPLE BRIE

Warm, melty brie and tart, crunchy apples — is there any better combination? Just add some savory chicken, and press the whole shebang in a panini press, and you've got yourself a sandwich! You don't have to be a celebrity chef to whip up this creation either. Leftover rotisserie chicken or sliced deli meat work just fine. Make sure to thinly slice your apples before laying them on so they'll get warm along with everything else.

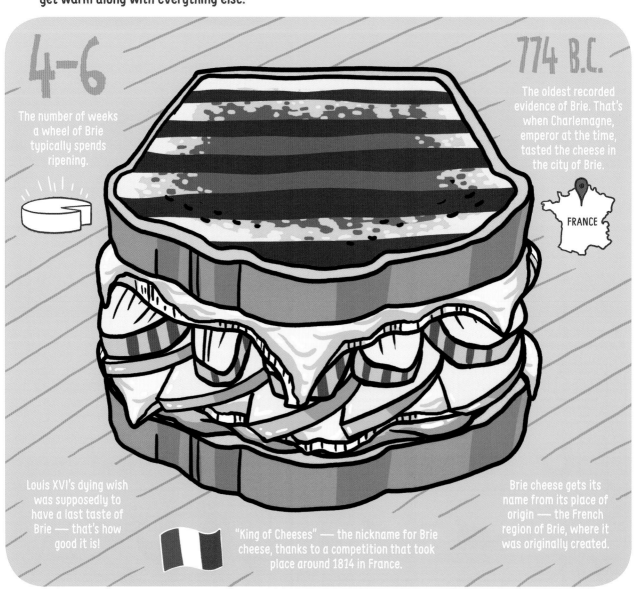

4-6
The number of weeks a wheel of Brie typically spends ripening.

774 B.C.
The oldest recorded evidence of Brie. That's when Charlemagne, emperor at the time, tasted the cheese in the city of Brie.

FRANCE

Louis XVI's dying wish was supposedly to have a last taste of Brie — that's how good it is!

"King of Cheeses" — the nickname for Brie cheese, thanks to a competition that took place around 1814 in France.

Brie cheese gets its name from its place of origin — the French region of Brie, where it was originally created.

SOURDOUGH BREAD

Serve with a side salad — or put the salad on your sandwich! Arugula or spinach would work well between the bread.

BRIE

Yes, you can eat the rind! The white outer layer of a wheel of brie is totally edible.

GRILLED CHICKEN

Try swapping leftover or sliced deli turkey for chicken — perfect as a post-Thanksgiving treat!

APPLES

If you're not crazy about apples — or you want to try something new — you can make this sandwich with peaches or figs.

BRIE

DIJON MUSTARD

HONEY MUSTARD

SOURDOUGH BREAD

No panini press? No problem! Just use a griddle or skillet and cook this one up like a standard grilled cheese.

CHICKEN APPLE BRIE

MEATLOAF

Meatloaf is a Midwestern dinner staple, and it's just as good the day after, especially when it's made with ground turkey, which is extra moist and delicious. All you need to whip up this tasty treat is access to leftovers! Try a cold turkey meatloaf sandwich — soft white bread, leftover turkey meatloaf, and a little mayo — or experiment with this hot version, complete with melty mozzarella and marinara sauce. You could also use veggie loaf here, depending on your personal preference.

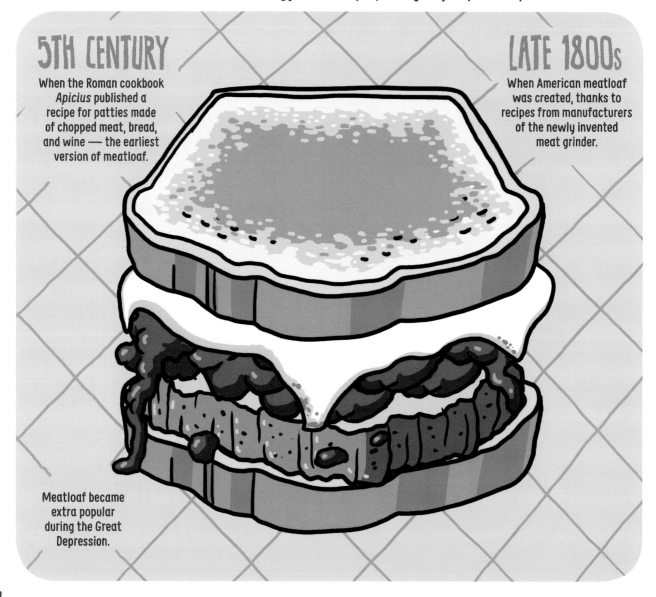

5TH CENTURY

When the Roman cookbook *Apicius* published a recipe for patties made of chopped meat, bread, and wine — the earliest version of meatloaf.

LATE 1800s

When American meatloaf was created, thanks to recipes from manufacturers of the newly invented meat grinder.

Meatloaf became extra popular during the Great Depression.

WHITE BREAD

MOZZARELLA CHEESE

MARINARA SAUCE

TURKEY MEATLOAF

WHITE BREAD

Serve with mashed potatoes, just like a real meatloaf dinner! Feeling extra adventurous? Add the mashed potatoes and gravy to your sandwich!

Cranberry relish makes a meatloaf sandwich sweet.

Add:

LETTUCE

TOMATO

SAUTÉED ONIONS

ARUGULA

TURKEY BACON

Grill your sandwich for a couple minutes on each side, until the bread is golden-brown and the toppings are gooey.

Plain old mayo or butter on the outside help this sandwich grill up nicely! (You can also skip the grilling altogether if you'd prefer.)

MEATLOAF

PATTY MELT

Not sure what to do with the leftover turkey burgers from your BBQ? Turn them into patty melts! While patty melts are typically made with hamburger, our version uses a turkey burger instead for an easy, delicious change of pace. Butter the bread and grill this one up, just like a grilled cheese. The only difference is the meat and onions in the middle!

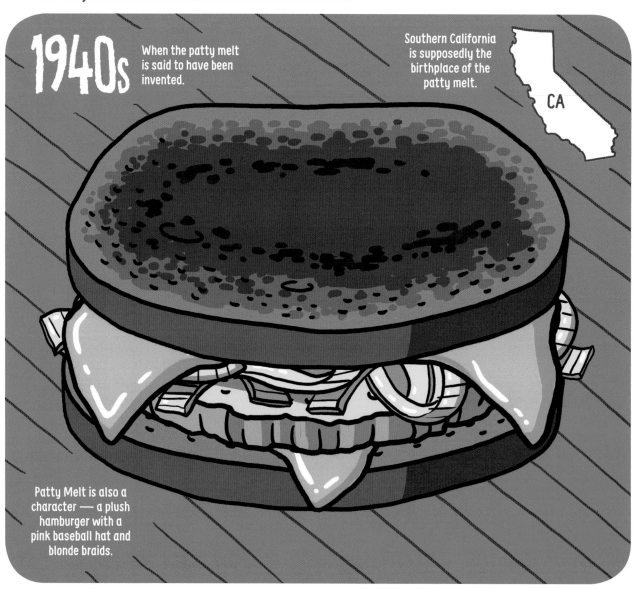

1940s When the patty melt is said to have been invented.

Southern California is supposedly the birthplace of the patty melt.

CA

Patty Melt is also a character — a plush hamburger with a pink baseball hat and blonde braids.

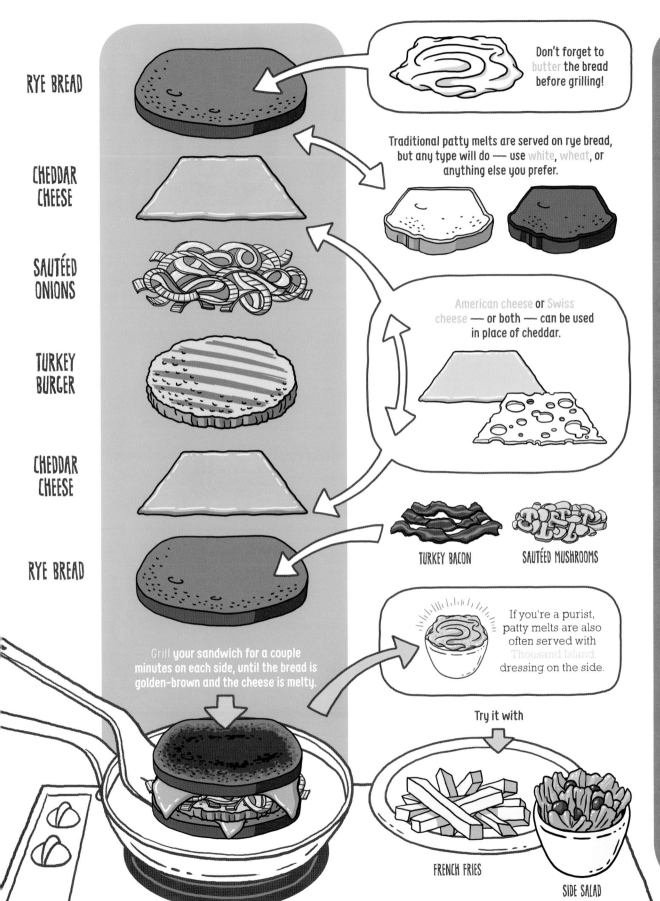

RYE BREAD

CHEDDAR CHEESE

SAUTÉED ONIONS

TURKEY BURGER

CHEDDAR CHEESE

RYE BREAD

Don't forget to butter the bread before grilling!

Traditional patty melts are served on rye bread, but any type will do — use white, wheat, or anything else you prefer.

American cheese or Swiss cheese — or both — can be used in place of cheddar.

TURKEY BACON

SAUTÉED MUSHROOMS

If you're a purist, patty melts are also often served with Thousand Island dressing on the side.

Grill your sandwich for a couple minutes on each side, until the bread is golden-brown and the cheese is melty.

Try it with

FRENCH FRIES

SIDE SALAD

PATTY MELT

31

RACHEL (TURKEY REUBEN)

A simpler, lighter version of a traditional reuben sandwich, "The Rachel" swaps out corned beef for turkey breast — perfect for those of us who don't eat red meat. Use leftover turkey if you have it — if not, sliced deli turkey will work just fine. This is a sandwich best served warm. Butter the outside of both slices of bread and toss it in a skillet for a couple of minutes on each side to warm the meat and melt the cheese before enjoying.

Despite its name, Russian dressing actually originated in the United States. It was invented by James E. Colburn of Nashua, New Hampshire.

In 2012, the average American ate 16 pounds of turkey.

A sandwich by any other name tastes just as sweet — the turkey reuben is also referred to as "The Robin" or a "Georgia Rueben."

RYE BREAD

THOUSAND
ISLAND
DRESSING

SWISS
CHEESE

COLESLAW

SLICED
TURKEY

SWISS
CHEESE

RYE BREAD

Don't forget to butter the bread before grilling!

Lightly toast your bread to keep the sandwich from getting soggy.

VS.

THOUSAND ISLAND VS. RUSSIAN DRESSING

Both types of dressing are known to have been added to the "The Rachel." So what's the difference? Both Russian and Thousand Island are mayonnaise-based and include ketchup. The main difference between the two is hard-boiled egg, which is typically found only in Thousand Island dressing. Russian dressing also tends to have a bolder flavor, while Thousand Island contains more vegetables.

There are several different versions of "The Rachel" — some call for traditional sauerkraut in place of coleslaw.

Grill your sandwich for a couple minutes on each side, until the bread is golden-brown and the toppings are gooey.

Try making mini Rachel sandwiches on pretzel rolls!

TURKEY PARMESAN

A turkey twist on the classic chicken parmesan, this grilled sandwich has all the makings of a new classic — savory turkey, TWO types of cheese, and marinara sauce to top it all off. Don't forget to butter the outsides of the bread before grilling to ensure they get extra crispy and golden-brown during the grilling process.

Melanzane alla parmigiana — which roughly translates to eggplant parmesan — is a southern Italian creation, but chicken parmesan was actually invented in the United States by Italian immigrants.

DID YOU KNOW?
Parmesan is also known as "Parmigiano Reggiano" which indicates the region of Italy it comes from, Parma and Reggio Emilia.

ITALY

Parmesan is the #3 bestselling cheese in the United States, after mozzarella and cheddar.

BREAD

Don't forget to butter the bread before grilling!

PROVOLONE CHEESE

Try substituting mozzarella for provolone cheese.

SHREDDED PARMESEAN

MARINARA SAUCE

AMP IT UP!
Add avocado or turkey bacon to your sandwich to make it even more delicious.

TURKEY

PROVOLONE CHEESE

CUSTOMIZE IT!

Any type of sliced sandwich bread will work for this sandwich — anything your stomach desires!

GARLIC TOAST

WHITE

BREAD

MULTI-GRAIN

WHEAT

Grill your sandwich for a couple minutes on each side, until the bread is golden-brown and the toppings are gooey.

ITALIAN ROLL

ENGLISH MUFFIN

TUNA SALAD

Tuna salad is just about as easy as cooking gets. All you really need is canned tuna and mayonnaise and you've got yourself a meal. Use less mayo if you prefer a drier tuna salad, or use more for a smoother, creamier texture. Add some salt and pepper, and voilà! If you're feeling fancy, try adding pickle relish or hardboiled eggs.

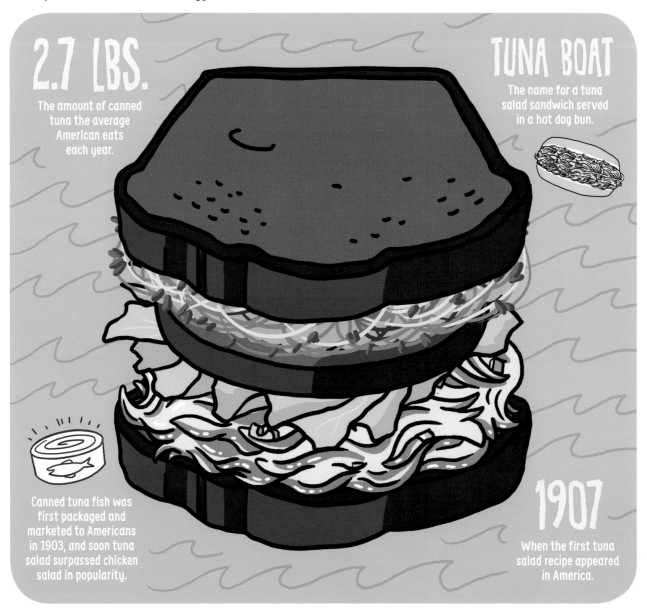

2.7 LBS.
The amount of canned tuna the average American eats each year.

TUNA BOAT
The name for a tuna salad sandwich served in a hot dog bun.

Canned tuna fish was first packaged and marketed to Americans in 1903, and soon tuna salad surpassed chicken salad in popularity.

1907
When the first tuna salad recipe appeared in America.

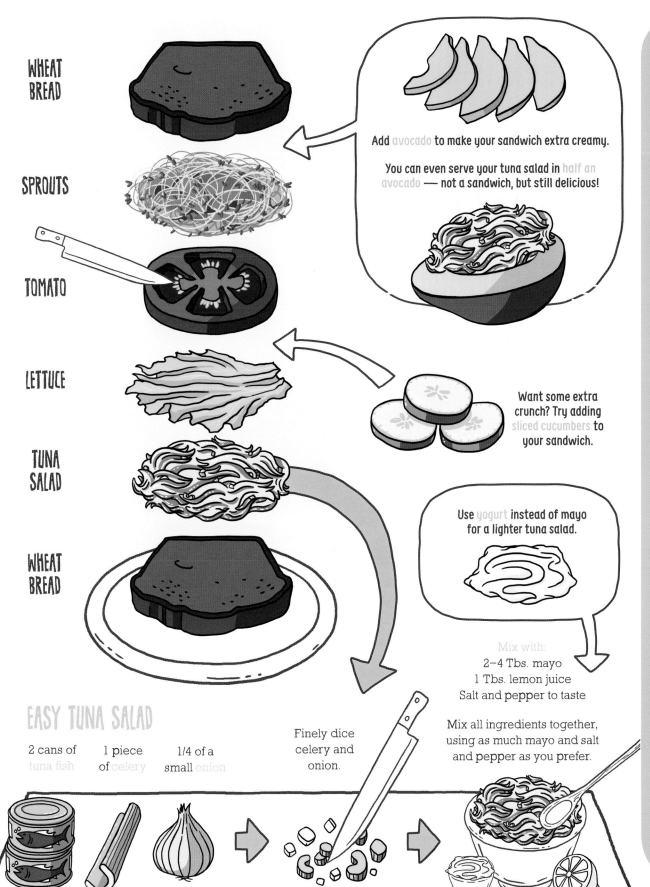

WHEAT BREAD

SPROUTS

TOMATO

LETTUCE

TUNA SALAD

WHEAT BREAD

Add avocado to make your sandwich extra creamy.

You can even serve your tuna salad in half an avocado — not a sandwich, but still delicious!

Want some extra crunch? Try adding sliced cucumbers to your sandwich.

Use yogurt instead of mayo for a lighter tuna salad.

Mix with:
2–4 Tbs. mayo
1 Tbs. lemon juice
Salt and pepper to taste

EASY TUNA SALAD

2 cans of tuna fish   1 piece of celery   1/4 of a small onion

Finely dice celery and onion.

Mix all ingredients together, using as much mayo and salt and pepper as you prefer.

TUNA MELT

Tuna salad not enough for you? Take your tuna sandwich to the next level by turning up the heat — literally. Whip up your basic tuna salad, then pile it onto your base of choice and top the whole thing with cheese. Pop it into the oven or toaster oven to make things melty, and then enjoy!

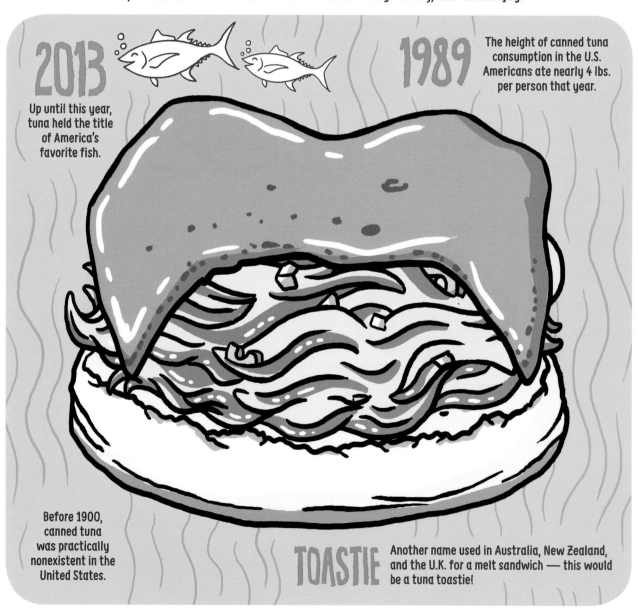

2013 Up until this year, tuna held the title of America's favorite fish.

1989 The height of canned tuna consumption in the U.S. Americans ate nearly 4 lbs. per person that year.

Before 1900, canned tuna was practically nonexistent in the United States.

TOASTIE Another name used in Australia, New Zealand, and the U.K. for a melt sandwich — this would be a tuna toastie!

CHEDDAR
CHEESE

TUNA
SALAD

ENGLISH
MUFFIN

This tuna melt is served open-faced, but you can easily use both halves of the English muffin if you prefer.

Use the recipe on the previous spread to make the tuna salad for this recipe.

Substitute one of these breads in place of the English muffin. (And just like the English muffin, you can add a second slice of bread if you prefer.)

WHITE

WHEAT

SOURDOUGH

RYE

Once you've assembled your tuna melt, a few minutes under the broiler will do the trick!

TIMER
2:50   BROIL   HI

Toast your English muffin — or bread if you prefer — before piling on the tuna salad and cheese.

TUNA MELT

39

CHICKEN SALAD

Can a salad and a sandwich ever coexist? In this case they can! Chicken salad is easy to make using leftover chicken. Don't have any in the fridge? A rotisserie chicken from the grocery store works just as well. And the beauty of this salad-sandwich hybrid is it can be eaten cold. Just whip up your chicken salad in advance, pile it onto your bread of choice, and eat! Easy to assemble and even easier to enjoy.

RI

1863

The year that the first American version of chicken salad was created. Liam Gray, founder of Town Meats in Wakefield, Rhode Island, mixed his leftover chicken with mayo, tarragon, and grapes, and voilà! Chicken salad was born. His creation was so popular the meat market turned into a deli.

The Chinese get the credit for creating chicken salad — they paired chicken with spices, oils, and binding substances.

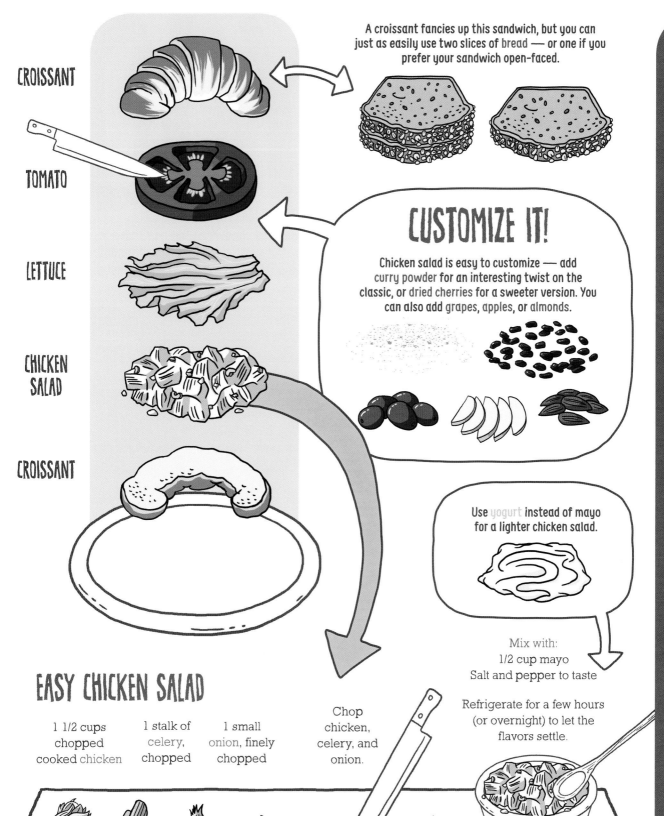

CROISSANT

A croissant fancies up this sandwich, but you can just as easily use two slices of bread — or one if you prefer your sandwich open-faced.

TOMATO

LETTUCE

CUSTOMIZE IT!

Chicken salad is easy to customize — add curry powder for an interesting twist on the classic, or dried cherries for a sweeter version. You can also add grapes, apples, or almonds.

CHICKEN SALAD

CROISSANT

Use yogurt instead of mayo for a lighter chicken salad.

Mix with:
1/2 cup mayo
Salt and pepper to taste

Refrigerate for a few hours (or overnight) to let the flavors settle.

EASY CHICKEN SALAD

| 1 1/2 cups chopped cooked chicken | 1 stalk of celery, chopped | 1 small onion, finely chopped |

Chop chicken, celery, and onion.

You can also add other herbs or spices to "spice" up the mixture.

41

SLOPPY JOE

Sloppy, savory, delicious — all the hallmarks of a truly awesome sandwich. And no sandwich embodies those attributes better than a good ol' sloppy joe. Our version is made with ground turkey to make the sandwich extra moist (and healthy!), but you can substitute ground chicken instead, or use ground beef if you eat red meat.

1933

CUBA

HAVANA, CUBA
Home of the original Sloppy Joe's Bar

Originally, mixing ground meat with sauces was a way to make it last longer — especially helpful during WWII.

The year Sloppy Joe's Bar opened in Key West, Florida — they've been serving sloppy joes ever since.

MARCH 18
National Sloppy Joe Day.

1969
The year Hunt's introduced Manwich — aka sloppy joe sauce in a can.

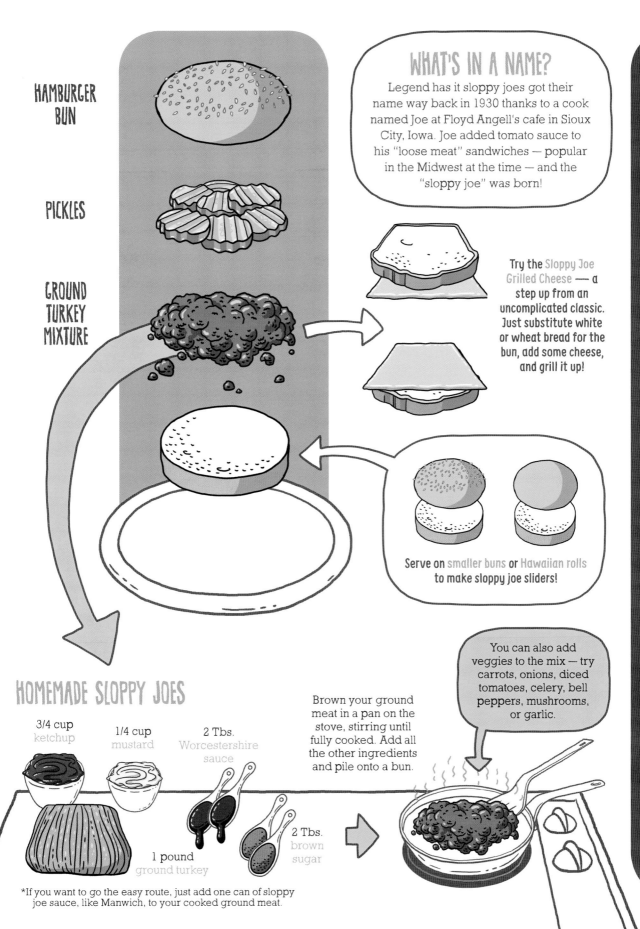

HAMBURGER BUN

PICKLES

GROUND TURKEY MIXTURE

WHAT'S IN A NAME?
Legend has it sloppy joes got their name way back in 1930 thanks to a cook named Joe at Floyd Angell's cafe in Sioux City, Iowa. Joe added tomato sauce to his "loose meat" sandwiches — popular in the Midwest at the time — and the "sloppy joe" was born!

Try the Sloppy Joe Grilled Cheese — a step up from an uncomplicated classic. Just substitute white or wheat bread for the bun, add some cheese, and grill it up!

Serve on smaller buns **or** Hawaiian rolls to make sloppy joe sliders!

You can also add veggies to the mix — try carrots, onions, diced tomatoes, celery, bell peppers, mushrooms, or garlic.

HOMEMADE SLOPPY JOES

Brown your ground meat in a pan on the stove, stirring until fully cooked. Add all the other ingredients and pile onto a bun.

3/4 cup ketchup

1/4 cup mustard

2 Tbs. Worcestershire sauce

1 pound ground turkey

2 Tbs. brown sugar

*If you want to go the easy route, just add one can of sloppy joe sauce, like Manwich, to your cooked ground meat.

PO' BOY

A southern staple, the po' boy comes to us from deep in the heart of Louisiana — New Orleans, to be specific. A traditional po' boy is made with fried seafood — shrimp, oysters, crab, and crawfish are all possibilities — and can be served hot or cold. A po' boy can also be made with roast beef. But no matter the filling, a po' boy is always served on a French baguette, crispy on the outside and soft in the center.

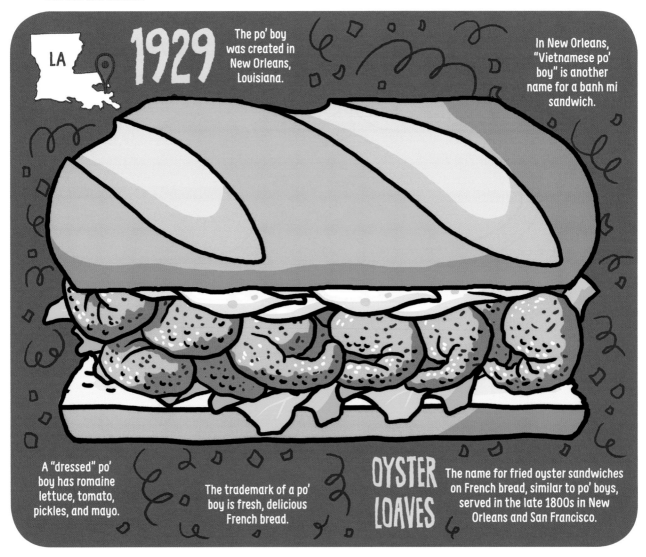

LA

1929 The po' boy was created in New Orleans, Louisiana.

In New Orleans, "Vietnamese po' boy" is another name for a banh mi sandwich.

A "dressed" po' boy has romaine lettuce, tomato, pickles, and mayo.

The trademark of a po' boy is fresh, delicious French bread.

OYSTER LOAVES The name for fried oyster sandwiches on French bread, similar to po' boys, served in the late 1800s in New Orleans and San Francisco.

TOASTED
BAGUETTE

RÉMOULADE
SAUCE

CAJUN
SEASONING

FRIED
SHRIMP

LETTUCE

TOASTED
BAGUETTE

ALL ABOUT THE PO' BOY

The name po' boy is a shortened version of "poor boy" and refers to the fact that the sandwich was originally a very inexpensive way to get a solid, filling meal. So who coined the term, and why? That would be Benny and Clovis Martin, brothers, restaurant owners, and former streetcar conductors in New Orleans. In 1929, approximately 1,800 transit workers went on strike for four months against the streetcar company. The Martin brothers served their former colleagues, who were protesting in the streets, sandwiches free of charge. Restaurant workers jokingly referred to the striking workers as "poor boys" and soon the name was stuck to the sandwiches as well.

Leftover fried shrimp works just fine, or use you can use frozen popcorn shrimp.

Try these other fillings too!

OYSTERS

CRAWFISH

CRAB

Brush the cut sides of your baguette with melted butter before toasting.

RÉMOULADE SAUCE

You can buy rémoulade sauce to drizzle on your po' boy, but if you want to go all in, it's easy to make your own!

1/2 cup mayo

1 Tbs. horseradish

1 tsp. pickle relish

1 tsp. minced garlic

1 tsp. cayenne pepper

Mix all ingredients together in a bowl. Drizzle over your sandwich and refrigerate the rest.

PO' BOY

45

BANH MI

This Vietnamese favorite features loads of fresh herbs and pickled veggies all crammed into a warm, toasty French baguette. And you can't argue that the sandwich isn't accurately named — *banh mi* is a Vietnamese term for all types of bread. This version uses grilled chicken, but a banh mi sandwich can also be made with beef or pork if you prefer. You can even use tofu if you're meat-free. Whatever your protein preference may be, this cultural sandwich is a guaranteed flavor explosion in your mouth.

3/24/2011   The date "banh mi" was added to the *Oxford English Dictionary*.

A banh mi has also been called a Vietnamese po' boy.

Cilantro is a must-have on a banh mi sandwich, but a good chunk of Americans think it tastes like soap.

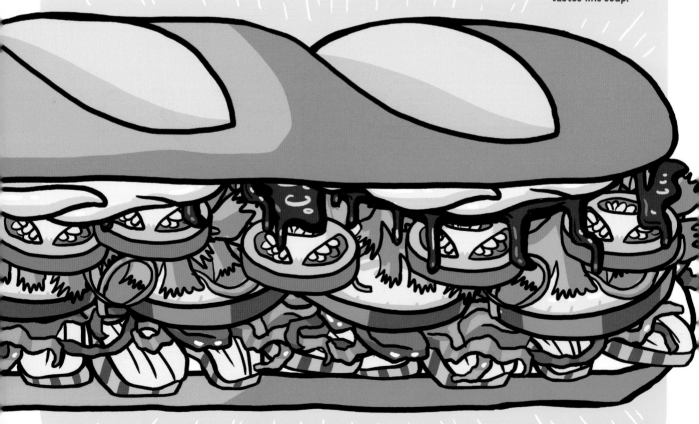

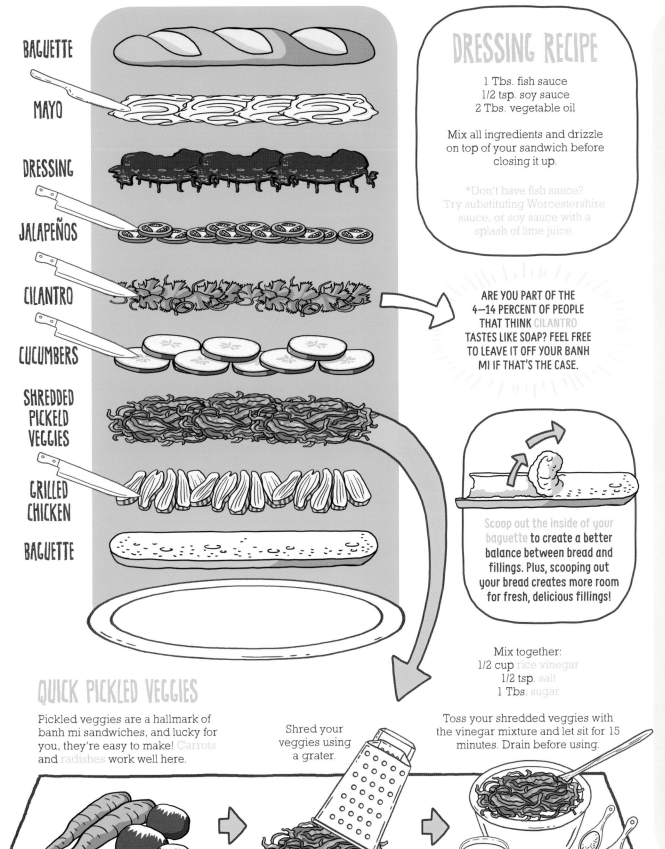

BAGUETTE

MAYO

DRESSING

JALAPEÑOS

CILANTRO

CUCUMBERS

SHREDDED
PICKLED
VEGGIES

GRILLED
CHICKEN

BAGUETTE

DRESSING RECIPE

1 Tbs. fish sauce
1/2 tsp. soy sauce
2 Tbs. vegetable oil

Mix all ingredients and drizzle on top of your sandwich before closing it up.

*Don't have fish sauce? Try substituting Worcestershire sauce, or soy sauce with a splash of lime juice.

ARE YOU PART OF THE 4–14 PERCENT OF PEOPLE THAT THINK CILANTRO TASTES LIKE SOAP? FEEL FREE TO LEAVE IT OFF YOUR BANH MI IF THAT'S THE CASE.

Scoop out the inside of your baguette to create a better balance between bread and fillings. Plus, scooping out your bread creates more room for fresh, delicious fillings!

Mix together:
1/2 cup rice vinegar
1/2 tsp. salt
1 Tbs. sugar

Toss your shredded veggies with the vinegar mixture and let sit for 15 minutes. Drain before using.

QUICK PICKLED VEGGIES

Pickled veggies are a hallmark of banh mi sandwiches, and lucky for you, they're easy to make! Carrots and radishes work well here.

Shred your veggies using a grater.

BANH MI

ALISON DEERING, AUTHOR

Originally from Michigan — the Mitten State! — Alison learned the value of a good book and a great sandwich early on. After earning a journalism degree from the University of Missouri-Columbia, she started her career as a writer and editor. Alison currently lives in Chicago, Illinois, with her husband, where she makes, eats, and talks about as many sandwiches as humanly possible.

If Alison were a sandwich, she would be a fancy grilled cheese, inspired by the Grilled 3 Cheese at Café Muse in Royal Oak, Michigan.

WHOLE GRAIN BREAD

HAVARTI CHEESE

TOMATO

BASIL

HONEY

FONTINA CHEESE

MOZZARELLA CHEESE

WHOLE GRAIN BREAD

BOB LENTZ, ILLUSTRATOR

Bob is an art director who has designed and illustrated many successful books for children, and is the latter half of the duo Lemke & Lentz, creators of *Book-O-Beards*, part of the Wearable Books series. In his spare time, he likes to talk about food, especially sandwiches. Bob lives in Minnesota, with his wife and children, where they go for long walks, sing old-timey songs, and eat ice cream with too many toppings.

If Bob were a sandwich, he would be "The Snowpig," proudly hailing from Morty's at Hyland Hills Ski Area in Bloomington, Minnesota.

FRENCH BREAD

SRIRACHA

SWEET AND SPICY PICKLES

APPLESAUCE

PROVOLONE CHEESE

PULLED PORK

FRENCH BREAD

READ MORE

Chandler, Jenny. *Great Food for Kids: Delicious Recipes and Fabulous Facts to Turn You Into a Kitchen Whiz*. San Francisco, Cali.: Weldon Owen, 2017.

Deering, Alison. *Hold the Meat: Vegetarian Sandwiches for Kids*. Between the Bread. North Mankato, Minn.: Capstone Press, 2017.

Hoena, Blake and Katrina Jorgensen. *Ballpark Cookbook The American League: Recipes Inspired by Baseball Stadium Foods*. Sports Illustrated Kids. North Mankato, Minn.: Capstone Press, 2016.

Use FACTHOUND to find Internet sites related to this book. Just type in 9781515739203 AND GO!